Date Due

Mama & Papa Have a Store

story and pictures by Amelia Lau Carling

Dial Books for Young Readers New York

Remembering Mama and Papa
As a young couple in 1938 when World War II was beginning,
my parents fled the Japanese invasion of their village
of Nine Rivers on the lush Pearl River delta in Guangdong, China.
Like other *paisanos,* countrymen from their own land,
they settled in Spanish-speaking Guatemala.

Although they both longed to return,
Mama never revisited Nine Rivers, but as a widower Papa
traveled back forty-five years later. In celebration, he set off
firecrackers at his parents' gravesites and, reunited with relatives,
feasted on the foods of his beloved hometown.

Published by Dial Books for Young Readers
A member of Penguin Putnam Inc.
375 Hudson Street • New York, New York 10014

Copyright © 1998 by Amelia Lau Carling
All rights reserved • Design and typography by Amelia Lau Carling
Printed in Hong Kong on acid-free paper
Chinese calligraphy on page 6 by Yang Ming-Yi
First Edition
1   3   5   7   9   10   8   6   4   2

Library of Congress Cataloging in Publication Data
Carling, Amelia Lau.
Mama and Papa have a store/story and pictures by Amelia Lau Carling.
—1st ed. p.   cm.
Summary: A little girl describes what a day is like in her parents'
Chinese store in Guatemala City.
ISBN 0-8037-2044-0 (trade).—ISBN 0-8037-2045-9 (lib. bdg.)
[1. Stores, Retail—Fiction. 2. Chinese—Fiction. 3. Guatemala—Fiction.] I. Title.
PZ7.L73019Mam 1998   [E]—dc21   97-10217   CIP   AC

The artwork was rendered in watercolor and gouache.

For

SuLin and Ana MeiLi,

and for

their cousins everywhere

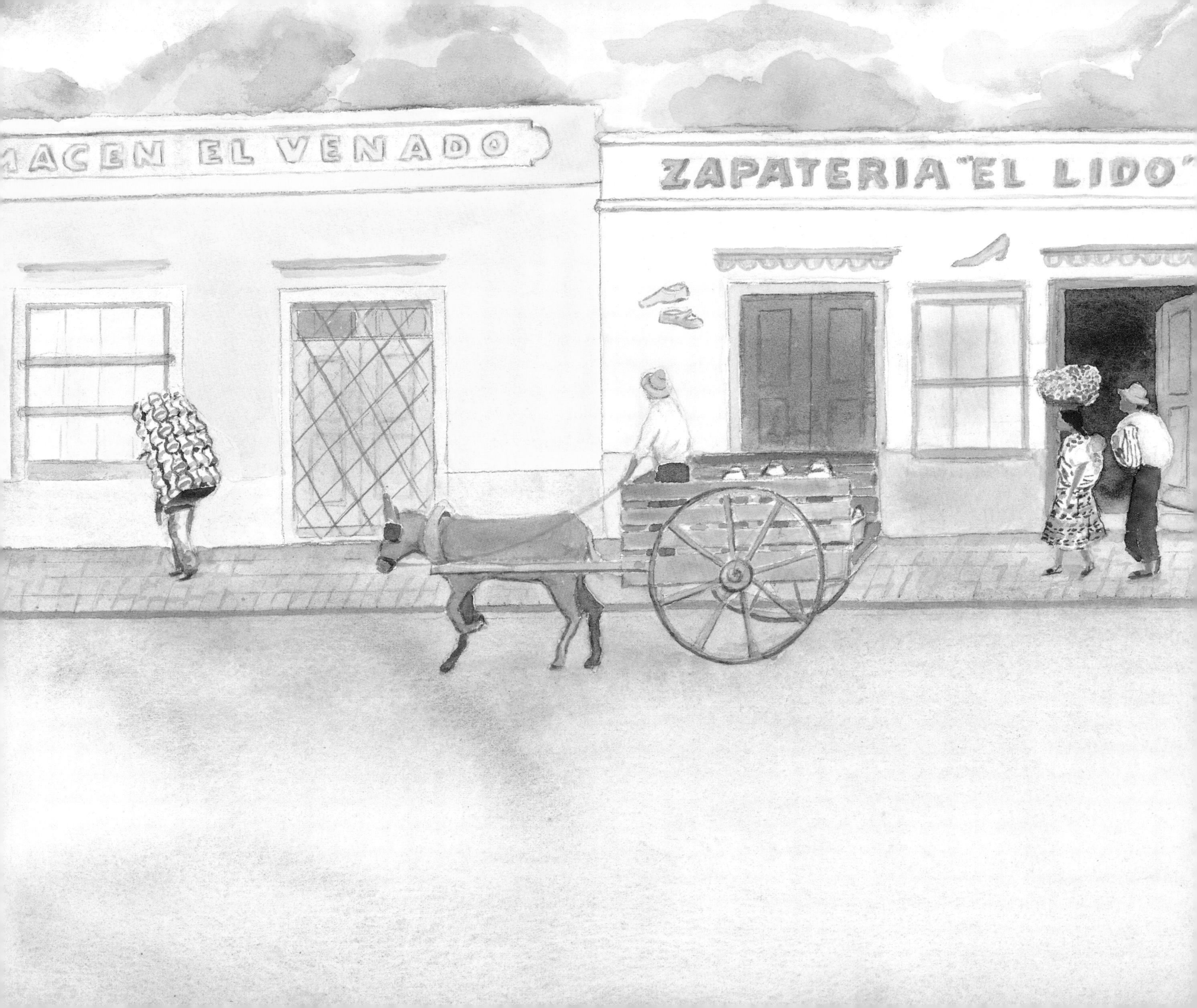
MACEN EL VENADO
ZAPATERIA "EL LIDO"

Clip, clop, clop. I hear the milkman and his mule cart. He rings our bell and leaves two bottles at the door.

Clip, clop, clop. The mule goes down the street. The church bells ring, the roosters crow. My brothers and sisters leave for school. The day begins like this.

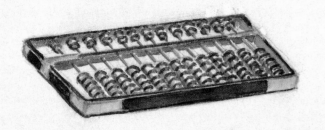

Mama and Papa have a store, a Chinese store in Guatemala City. They sell buttons, ribbons, thread, and cloth. They sell paper lanterns, plastic balls, firecrackers, and perfume. Needles, white gloves, tablecloths, bottles of soy sauce—there's everything in my parents' store. It smells of flowers and of the freshly swept moist sawdust they use for cleaning the tiled floor.

Mama knits without looking down and talks with the customers in Spanish. They call her doña Graciela. But in Chinese her name means Lady Who Lives in the Moon.

Papa at his desk adds and subtracts with his abacus. He is don Rodolfo in Spanish, and in Chinese his name means Fragrant Pond.

劉澤芬 曾肖嫦

From the stoop I watch the street.

"*¡Buenos días!*"

Don Chus sets up pictures of saints along the wall. I look for the one that shows good people led by angels toward heaven and bad people led by devils toward the flames of hell.

El ciego, the blind man, sells lottery tickets. I've seen Mama choose her lucky numbers and buy ten tickets at a time. Once she won the rolling cart that she keeps in the dining room.

La chiclera, the candy woman, arranges neat rows of sweets in a wooden box. When Mama and Papa let me have five *centavos*, I buy enough to fill my pockets.

Santiago and María and their daughter Elsita are here today. They've come in a bus from an Indian village far away. I've heard them tell Mama that they, like their parents and their grandparents before them, live on the edge of a lake surrounded by three volcanoes. Imagine that!

They come to buy thread to weave their clothes. María leans over the counter and looks at the rows and rows of colored strands arranged like schools of fish in glassy water.

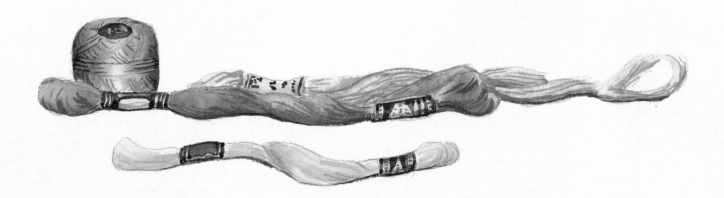

In imperfect Spanish she says, "Parrot green, sky blue, pomegranate red, fire orange, loud magenta, and mango yellow—those are the colors from the rain forest that we want."

She will weave deer, birds, rabbits, and jaguars into new clothes.
I know, because with my eyes I've often played games on the patterns woven into the clothing of the Indians who come to the store.

"Stained maroon, iguana green, ocean blue, sunset yellow—those are the colors from the marshes that we want."

She will weave water, thunder, lightning, and flowers into new clothes.

"Volcano purple, maize yellow, hot pepper red—those are the colors from the cornfields that we want."

She will weave boys with straw hats and girls with baskets on their heads.

Don Chema, the Chinese bean curd seller, brings fresh tofu. Mama buys some and invites him to sit down for a cup of tea poured from a thermos, the kind she sells in the store.

Mama, Papa, and don Chema chat loudly in Chinese, laughing and shouting. They talk about Nine Rivers, their hometown in China— who stayed, who left, how fresh the fish was, and which dishes they haven't had since they fled more than fifteen years ago, and how they lost their homes in a terrible war. They complain how slow the mail is for sending money back.

It's time to close for lunch. Nena, Beto, Mando, Chiki, and Adolfo are back from school. The Indian family leaves to eat and nap at the marketplace, a block away.

We'll eat right here, because we live in the back of the store. Mama's already in the kitchen cleaning fish, slicing hot peppers, mincing meat with two cleavers. *Taka, taka, chomp. Taka, taka, chomp.*

Beto calls us to feed the goldfish in the *pila*, a pool of water in the middle of our patio. The fish hide among the plants in the bottom, but dart out of the deep green when the bread crumbs fall on the water.

The fire roars in the wood-burning stove. Food sizzles in the wok, and Mama sets dish after dish next to a pile of corn tortillas. Mama, Papa, and don Chema, who often stays for lunch, talk about uncles, aunts, friends, and cousins from Nine Rivers, Hong Kong, and Taiwan. These are people and places so far away, I know of them only by the old photographs and pictures on the calendars hung around the house. But my brothers and sisters and I don't pay much attention.

We're eager to finish eating and go up to the roof terrace.

La terraza is up an old rickety staircase near the kitchen.

That's where Papa plants roses and Chinese lilies in leftover wooden crates and has a miniature landscape of a cement mountain with little pagodas and red goldfish that swim around it.

"This is the famous Yellow Mountain in old China," he says. I imagine climbing the steep cliffs and getting lost among the craggy rocks. But how wonderful to cross a moon bridge and rest beside a pagoda!

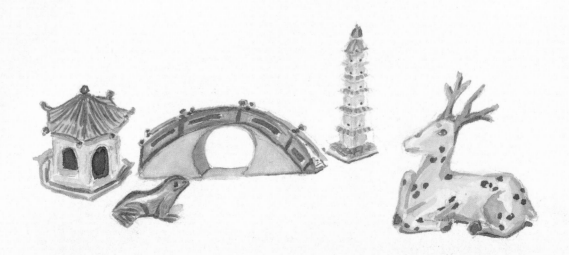

We climb the roof—it's safe to climb on. With candles Nena, Beto, Mando, and I rub wax on the tin roof. Then, with cardboard sleds we glide again and again, laughing and spilling against the wall at the bottom.

A gray cloud moves in and sprinkles rain. There's a rainbow in the sunny sky!

But Mama calls my brothers and sisters to go back to school. Don Chema has gone home. Mama puts powder and lipstick on her face. Papa puts on a jacket and opens the store again. The Indian family is already waiting at the door.

"*¡Buenas tardes!*"

People come and go in the long afternoon.

Dark, dark clouds sweep in quickly, taking the sun away and letting large raindrops fall hard on the tin roof. *Pong, pong, pong.* The sound above my head rises, then softens, then rises. Papa flicks on the lights. "It's already dark at three in the afternoon!" he says.

The rain pelts the roof. It's so loud, people have to raise their voices to be heard.

When my brothers and sisters come home from school, we make paper boats and float them down the street.

Then they set up their books on the counter and do their homework. Suddenly the lights go out. That happens when it rains a lot. Papa gets the gas-lamps and pumps them while we hold the flashlights. He hangs the lanterns above the counters, and with our fingers we make large shadow puppets.

Mama goes to the kitchen to make supper by lantern light while Papa minds the store.

Suddenly the lights come back. Santiago and María tie their boxes of thread into bundles. He carries one on his back. She and Elsita each carry one on her head. They must hurry to catch the last bus back to their village.

It's time to begin closing the store. The rain slows to a drizzle. Santiago, María, and Elsita are the last to leave.

"*¡Buenas noches!*"

Papa covers the display window out in front. Then he closes all the doors and pulls the iron gates shut.

Clic, clac, clac. Papa counts money with his abacus. On a small black stone he grinds black ink, and with a Chinese brush he writes Chinese words in columns, from right to left, on the soft paper of his accounting book. Mama finishes her knitting. My brothers and sisters are inside getting ready for tomorrow.

I sing and dance on the tiled floor. I'm sure Papa and Mama watch out of the corner of an eye. *Clic, clac, clac*. This is how the day ends.